Delicious
wraps

Delicious
wraps

Love Food™ is an imprint of Parragon Books Ltd

Parragon
Queen Street House
4 Queen Street
Bath BA1 1HE

Introduction by Frances Eames
Photography by Günter Beer
Food Styling by Stevan Paul

ISBN 978-1-4054-9561-5

Printed in China

Notes for reader
• This book uses imperial, metric, and US cup measurements. Follow the same units
of measurement throughout; do not mix imperial and metric.
• All spoon measurements are level: teaspoons are assumed to be 5 ml and
tablespoons are assumed to be 15 ml.
• Unless otherwise stated, milk is assumed to be whole and eggs are medium. The
times given are an approximate guide only.
• Some recipes contain nuts. If you are allergic to nuts you should avoid using them
and any products containing nuts.
• Recipes using raw or very lightly cooked eggs should be avoided by infants, the
elderly, pregnant women, convalescents, and anyone suffering from illness.

Contents

Wraps

Wraps are the new take on that all-time favorite, the sandwich. They are light, bright, fun, and healthy—great for lunchboxes, light lunches, relaxed outdoor eating, or an informal dinner party with friends.

Wraps are big business these days and, although they seem to have appeared from nowhere, the wrap has a history of its own. Bobby Valentine, an American former baseball manager, is credited with the invention of the wrap sandwich at his Connecticut restaurant.

Variety

Wraps will satisfy both healthy eaters and those looking for a guilty pleasure. Whether or not you're on a low-calorie diet, wraps are definitely on the menu. They are easy to prepare and good for the whole family; they usually take only a few minutes to put together and so are ideal for lunchboxes. Variations in ingredients cater for all needs; for more fiber, substitute your normal wraps for whole wheat tortillas. Or, for wheat-free recipes, try corn tortillas instead.

Evening Entertaining

Wrap- and tortilla-based meals are perfect for a casual evening with friends. Mediterranean-inspired recipes are ideal for *al fresco* eating. You can offer several different fillings to accommodate vegetarians and meat-eaters with the minimum of fuss. With an array of fresh ingredients and bright colors, wraps look delicious and take little or no cooking. No wonder they are so popular!

Appetizers and Desserts

Wraps are even great to serve as appetizers or desserts. Why not try a modern twist on the traditional appetizers with a Shrimp & Avocado Wrap (see page 51)?

For those of you with a sweet tooth, crêpes and pancakes offer an easy and tasty dessert that can be whipped up in an instant, for example a simple Chocolate & Banana Crêpe (see page 83).

Children's Favorites

Children love wraps as they can eat them with their fingers. If you or your children are vegetarian and you are worried about eating enough vegetables, then wraps are a great way to encourage a wider variety of greens on the menu. Plus, half the fun with wraps is that you can really involve your children in the preparation of ingredients, plus the actual wrapping!

Wrapping—"the roll"

This is the easiest way. Simply place your filling in the center of the wrap and spread in a vertical line to the end of the top and bottom sides. Then either fold the left and right sides over the filling, or fold one side over the filling and roll the filled section over the other side. However, be careful not to drop the filling out of the end of the wrap.

"Open-ended"

This way you see the filling at one end but the other end is folded. This method is like creating a pocket. Place your filling in the center of the tortilla and spread in a vertical line to the end of the top side. Fold up the bottom third of the wrap over the filing. Take the left and right sides of the wrap (the part that has no filling on it) and fold them over the filling, creating an easy-to-eat pocket.

Don't forget to put out plenty of napkins for sticky fingers!

It's a Wrap!

makes 8

3 tbsp olive oil, plus extra for drizzling

3 tbsp maple syrup or honey

1 tbsp red wine vinegar

2 garlic cloves, crushed

2 tsp dried oregano

1–2 tsp dried red pepper flakes

salt and pepper

4 skinless, boneless chicken breasts

2 red bell peppers, seeded and cut into 1-inch/2.5-cm strips

8 flour tortillas, warmed

green salad and guacamole, to serve

chicken fajitas

Place the oil, maple syrup, vinegar, garlic, oregano, pepper flakes, and salt and pepper to taste in a large, shallow dish or bowl and mix together.

Slice the chicken across the grain into slices 1 inch/2.5 cm thick. Toss in the marinade until well coated. Cover and let chill in the refrigerator for 2–3 hours, turning occasionally.

Heat a broiler pan until hot. Lift the chicken slices from the marinade with a slotted spoon, lay on the broiler pan, and cook over medium-high heat for 3–4 minutes on each side, or until cooked through. Remove the chicken to a warmed serving plate and keep warm.

Add the bell peppers, skin-side down, to the broiler pan and cook for 2 minutes on each side. Transfer to the serving plate.

Serve at once with the warmed tortillas to be used as wraps.

makes 4

for the filling

2 medium chicken breasts

1 tbsp olive oil

2 eggs

4 x 10-inch/25-cm sun-dried
tomato wraps

4 Boston lettuce leaves,
washed

4 white anchovies

2 tbsp freshly grated
Parmesan cheese

salt and pepper

for the caesar dressing

3 tbsp mayonnaise

1 tbsp water

1/2 tbsp white wine vinegar

salt and pepper

caesar chicken wraps

Preheat the oven to 400°F/200°C.

Place the chicken breasts on a nonstick baking sheet, rub with the olive oil, and season with salt and pepper. Place in the oven and cook for 20 minutes. Remove from the oven and let cool.

Bring a small saucepan of water to a boil, add the eggs, and cook for 9 minutes, then cool under cold running water for 5 minutes. Once cooled, shell and roughly chop the eggs. Shred the chicken and combine with the chopped egg.

To make the dressing, put the mayonnaise, water, white wine vinegar and salt and pepper to taste in a screw-top jar and shake until blended. Combine with the chicken and egg and set aside.

Preheat a nonstick skillet or broiler pan until almost smoking, then add the wraps, 1 at a time, and cook for 10 seconds on each side. This will add some color and soften the wraps.

Place a lettuce leaf in the center of each wrap, then top with the chicken and egg mixture, anchovies, and cheese.

makes 4

4 x 10-inch/25-cm wraps

2 oz/55 g cranberry sauce

9 oz/255 g cooked turkey breast, shredded

5 1/2 oz/150 g brie, sliced

salt and pepper

turkey wraps with brie & cranberry

Preheat a nonstick skillet or broiler pan until almost smoking, add the wraps, 1 at a time, and cook for 10 seconds on each side. This will add some color and soften the wraps.

Spread the cranberry sauce evenly over the wraps and divide the turkey and brie evenly among them, placing some along the center of each wrap. Sprinkle with salt and pepper, then fold in the wraps at the ends. Roll up each wrap, cut in half diagonally, and serve.

makes 8

2 tbsp olive oil, plus extra
for oiling

2 large onions, thinly sliced

1 lb 4 oz/550 g lean beef, cut
into bite-size pieces

1 tbsp ground cumin

1–2 tsp cayenne pepper,
or to taste

1 tsp paprika

8 soft corn tortillas

1 quantity Taco Sauce,
warmed, and thinned with a
little water if necessary

8 oz/225 g Cheddar cheese,
grated

salt and pepper

to serve

avocado, diced

red onion, finely chopped

mustard

beef enchiladas

Preheat the oven to 350°F/180°C. Oil a large, rectangular baking dish.

Heat the oil in a large skillet over low heat. Add the onions and cook for 10 minutes, or until soft and golden. Remove with a slotted spoon and set aside.

Increase the heat to high, add the beef, and cook, stirring, for 2–3 minutes, or until browned on all sides. Reduce the heat to medium, add the spices and salt and pepper to taste, and cook, stirring constantly, for 2 minutes.

Warm each tortilla in a lightly oiled nonstick skillet for 15 seconds on each side, then dip each, in turn, in the sauce. Top with a little of the beef, onions, and grated cheese and roll up.

Place seam-side down in the prepared baking dish, top with the remaining sauce and grated cheese, and bake in the preheated oven for 20 minutes. Serve at once.

makes 4

9 oz/250 g sirloin steak

1 tbsp olive oil

4 1/2 oz/125 g bleu cheese,
such as Stilton, crumbled

1 tbsp mayonnaise

4 x 10-inch/25-cm wraps

a small bunch of fresh
watercress

salt and pepper

beef & bleu cheese wraps

Season the steak with salt and pepper.

Preheat a nonstick skillet until almost smoking. Add the oil, then add the steak and seal, cooking for 30 seconds on each side for very rare (or longer according to personal preference). Remove from the skillet and set aside to rest for a few minutes. Cut into thin strips with a sharp knife.

Mix together the cheese and mayonnaise.

Preheat a nonstick skillet or broiler pan until almost smoking, add the wraps, 1 at a time, and cook for 10 seconds on each side. This will add some color and soften the wraps.

Divide the steak strips evenly among the wraps, placing some along the center of each wrap. Top with some of the cheese and mayonnaise mixture, and then with some watercress. Fold in the wraps at the ends, roll up, cut in half diagonally, and serve.

makes 4

2 rump steaks, about
8 oz/225 g each

finely grated rind and
juice of 1 lime

1 fresh green chile, seeded
and finely chopped

2 garlic cloves, crushed

pinch of sugar

2 tbsp olive oil

1 small onion, thinly sliced

1 red bell pepper, thinly
sliced

4 wheat tortillas

salt and pepper

tomato salsa and sour cream,
to serve

steak & lime tortillas

Thinly slice the steaks. To make the marinade, put the lime rind and juice, chile, garlic, sugar, and salt and pepper to taste into a large, shallow, nonmetallic dish and mix together. Add the steak and turn in the marinade to coat it. Cover and let marinate in the refrigerator for 3–4 hours, turning occasionally.

Heat the oil in a large skillet over medium heat. Add the onion and red bell pepper and cook, stirring frequently, for 5 minutes until softened. Using a slotted spoon, remove the steak from the marinade, add to the skillet, and cook, stirring constantly, for 2–3 minutes until browned. Add the marinade, bring to a boil, and toss together.

Meanwhile, warm the tortillas according to the instructions on the package. Divide the steak mixture among the tortillas, then fold in one side and roll up each tortilla to form an open-ended container. Serve hot with tomato salsa and sour cream to spoon on top.

makes 4

½ duck, Chinese style

3 oz/85 g rhubarb

1 tbsp water

2 tsp white sugar

4 x 10-inch/25-cm multigrain
wraps

1 mango, peeled and sliced

4 scallions, cut into 2-inch/
5-cm pieces

a small bunch of cilantro

salt and pepper

crispy duck wraps with mango & rhubarb

Preheat the oven to 400°F/220°C.

Place the duck in the oven on a nonstick baking sheet and cook for 20–25 minutes, or until crisp. Remove from the oven and set aside to cool.

Heat the rhubarb in a small saucepan with the water and sugar and cook for about 5 minutes, or until the rhubarb starts to break down. Remove the pan from the heat and set aside to cool.

Pull all of the meat off the duck and shred.

Preheat a nonstick skillet or broiler pan until almost smoking, add the wraps, 1 at a time, and cook for 10 seconds on each side. This will add some color and soften the wraps.

Divide the duck, mango, and scallions evenly among the wraps, placing some along the center of each wrap. Sprinkle with salt and pepper and top with a spoonful of rhubarb and cilantro. Fold in each wrap at the ends, roll up, cut in half diagonally, and serve.

makes 4

11 oz/310 g lamb leg steak

1/2 tbsp olive oil

4 x 10-inch/25-cm wraps

3 1/2 oz/100 g canned piquillo peppers, drained and sliced

2 oz/55 g pitted green olives

a small bunch of fresh flat-leaf parsley

salt and pepper

for the aïoli

3 tbsp mayonnaise

1 tbsp extra-virgin olive oil

1 garlic clove, crushed

salt and pepper

lamb wraps with peppers & aioli

Rub the lamb with the olive oil and some salt and pepper.

Preheat a broiler pan until almost smoking, add the lamb to the pan, and and cook for 2–3 minutes on each side. The lamb should be pink in the middle. Remove the lamb from the pan and set aside in a warm place.

To make the aïoli, mix together the mayonnaise, olive oil, and garlic and season with salt and pepper to taste.

Slice the lamb into thin strips. Meanwhile, preheat the broiler to high.

Place the wraps on a nonstick baking sheet and place under the broiler for 1 minute.

Divide the lamb evenly among the wraps, placing some along the center of each.

Top the lamb with peppers, olives, and parsley and spoon over some aïoli. Roll up the wraps and serve.

makes 4

2 tsp mustard

2 oz/55 g thick apple sauce

4 x 10-inch/25-cm wraps

10 oz/280 g roast pork, shredded

3½ oz/100 g sharp Cheddar cheese, sliced

salt and pepper

roast pork wraps with apple & cheddar

Mix the mustard and apple sauce together and season with salt and pepper.

Preheat a nonstick skillet or broiler pan until almost smoking, add the wraps, 1 at a time, and cook for 10 seconds on each side. This will add some color and soften the wraps.

Divide the pork and cheese evenly among the wraps, placing some in the center of each wrap. Top with the mustard and apple sauce mixture. Fold in the wraps at the ends, roll up, cut in half diagonally, and serve.

makes 20

4 oz/115 g firm beancurd

3 tbsp vegetable or peanut oil

1 tsp finely chopped garlic

2 oz/55 g lean pork, shredded

4 oz/115 g raw shrimp, peeled and deveined

1/2 small carrot, cut into short thin sticks

1/2 cup fresh or canned bamboo shoots, rinsed and shredded (if using fresh shoots, boil in water first for 30 minutes)

1 cup very finely sliced cabbage

1/2 cup snow peas, julienned

1-egg omelet, shredded

1 tsp salt

1 tsp light soy sauce

1 tsp Shaoxing rice wine

pinch of white pepper

20 soft spring roll skins

chili bean sauce, to serve

soft-wrapped pork & shrimp rolls

Slice the beancurd into thin slices horizontally and cook in 1 tablespoon of the oil until it turns golden brown. Cut into thin strips and set aside.

In a preheated wok or deep pan, heat the remaining oil and stir-fry the garlic until fragrant. Add the pork and stir for about 1 minute, then add the shrimp and stir for an additional minute. One by one, stirring well after each, add the carrot, bamboo shoots, cabbage, snow peas, beancurd, and, finally, the shredded omelet. Season with the salt, light soy sauce, Shaoxing rice wine, and pepper. Stir for an additional minute, then turn into a serving dish.

To assemble each roll, smear a skin with a little chili bean sauce and place a heaped teaspoon of the filling toward the bottom of the circle. Roll up the bottom edge to secure the filling, turn in the sides, and continue to roll up gently.

Fisherman's Catch

makes 4

11 oz/310 g fresh salmon fillet

1 tbsp olive oil

salt and pepper

4 eggs

2 tbsp mayonnaise

2 tbsp sour cream

3/4 oz/20 g capers, chopped

zest of 1 lemon

a small bunch of fresh dill, chopped

4 x 10-inch/25-cm wraps

salmon & dill wraps

Preheat the oven to 400°F/200°C.

Place the salmon on a nonstick baking sheet. Brush with olive oil and season with salt and pepper to taste. Place in the oven and cook for 8–10 minutes. Remove from the oven and let cool.

Bring a small saucepan of water to a boil, add the eggs, and cook for 9 minutes, then cool under cold running water for 5 minutes. Shell the eggs and chop them roughly.

Flake the salmon into a bowl, removing any skin. Add the eggs, mayonnaise, sour cream, capers, lemon zest, and dill.

Preheat a nonstick skillet or broiler pan until almost smoking, add the wraps, 1 at a time, and cook for 10 seconds on each side. This will add some color and soften the wraps.

Divide the salmon mixture evenly among the wraps, placing some in the center of each wrap. Fold in each wrap at the ends, roll up, cut in half diagonally, and serve.

makes 4

for the omelets

4 eggs

2 tbsp water

3 scallions, finely chopped

2 tbsp fresh cilantro, finely chopped

1 tbsp groundnut or vegetable oil

soy sauce, to serve

for the filling

1 tbsp groundnut or vegetable oil

3 scallions, roughly chopped

8 oz/225 g raw squid, cleaned and cut into chunks if large or rings if small

4 oz/115 g raw shrimp, peeled and deveined

4 oz/115 g skinned white fish fillet, such as cod or coley, cut into 1-inch/2.5-cm cubes

1 head pak choi, roughly chopped

2 tbsp fresh cilantro, finely chopped

1 tbsp green curry paste

1 tsp Thai fish sauce

spicy Thai parcels

Preheat the oven to 375°F/190°C. For the omelets, beat the eggs, water, scallions and half the cilantro together in a bowl. Heat the oil in a 20-cm/8-inch nonstick skillet. Drizzle a quarter of the egg mixture over the base of the skillet to make a rough lacy pattern. Cook over medium–high heat for 2 minutes, or until just set, then use a palette knife to turn the omelet over and cook on the other side for 1 minute. Slide out onto a plate or chopping board. Repeat with the remaining mixture to make 3 more omelets and add to the plate or board.

For the filling, heat 1 tablespoon of oil in the skillet, add the scallions and all the seafood and cook over medium heat, stirring frequently, for 2–3 minutes until the squid is firm, the shrimp have turned pink and the fish is just cooked through. Transfer to a food processor and process for 30 seconds, or until just mixed. Add the pak choi, the cilantro, the curry paste, and fish sauce and process again to a coarse mixture.

Arrange the omelets on a chopping board and put a quarter of the seafood mixture in the centre of each. Roll one side of each omelet over the filling, fold in the adjacent 'sides' to cover the filling, then fold up the omelet to make a small, square parcel. Transfer the parcels to a baking sheet.

Bake in the preheated oven for 10–15 minutes until lightly browned and cooked through. Serve immediately with soy sauce.

makes 24

24 cooked tail-on (peeled and tails left intact) king shrimp

2 tbsp sweet chili dipping sauce

24 wonton wrappers

groundnut or vegetable oil, for deep-frying

for the dipping sauce

1 tbsp sesame oil

3 tbsp soy sauce

½-inch/1-cm piece fresh gingerroot, peeled and finely chopped

1 scallion, finely chopped

shrimp wraps

Toss the shrimp in the chili sauce in a bowl. Remove the wrappers from the packet, but keep them in a pile and covered with plastic wrap to prevent them drying out. Lay one wrapper on a work surface in front of you and brush the edges with water. Place a shrimp diagonally across the square and fold the wrapper around the shrimp to enclose it completely, leaving the tail extended. Repeat with the remaining wrappers and shrimp.

Heat the oil in a wok or a deep saucepan or deep-fat fryer to 180–190°C/350–375°F, or until a cube of bread browns in 30 seconds. Add the wraps, in batches, and cook for 45 seconds–1 minute until crisp and golden all over. Remove with a slotted spoon, drain on kitchen paper and keep warm while you cook the remaining wraps.

Meanwhile, to make the dipping sauce, mix the sesame oil, soy sauce, gingerroot, and scallion together in a bowl. Serve in small serving bowls with the wraps.

makes 4

4 x 10-inch/25-cm wraps

7 oz/200 g cooked crayfish tails

1 mango, peeled and sliced

½ cucumber, seeded and quartered

a small bunch of fresh mint

a small bunch of fresh cilantro

for the dressing

2 tbsp yogurt

1 tbsp mayonnaise

1 tsp medium curry paste

1 tsp mango chutney

salt and pepper

crayfish wraps with mango & cucumber

To make the dressing, mix all the dressing ingredients together.

Preheat a nonstick skillet or broiler pan until almost smoking, add the wraps, 1 at a time, and cook for 10 seconds on each side. This will add some color and soften the wraps.

Divide the crayfish tails evenly among the wraps, placing some in the center of each wrap, then top with some mango, cucumber, mint, and cilantro.

Spoon over the dressing, then fold up each wrap at the ends, roll up, cut into slices, and serve.

makes 4

7 oz/200 g canned tuna, drained

4 tbsp mayonnaise

2½ oz/70 g pitted green olives, chopped

4 scallions, sliced

a small bunch of fresh flat-leaf parsley, shredded

4 lettuce leaves, washed

4 x 10-inch/25-cm wraps

salt and pepper

tuna mayonnaise wraps with olives

Mix the tuna, mayonnaise, olives, scallions, and parsley together in a bowl, then season with salt and pepper to taste.

Preheat a nonstick skillet or broiler pan until almost smoking, add the wraps, 1 at a time, and cook for 10 seconds on each side. This will add some color and soften the wraps.

Place a lettuce leaf in the center of each wrap, then divide the tuna mixture evenly among the wraps, placing some on top of each lettuce leaf. Fold in the wraps at the ends, roll up, cut in half diagonally, and serve.

makes 4

8 oz/255 g baby fennel

5½ oz/150 g fresh or canned white crabmeat

4 tbsp mayonnaise

zest and juice of 1 lemon

a small bunch of fresh flat-leaf parsley, shredded

4 x 10-inch/25-cm Mediterranean herb wraps

salt and pepper

crab & fennel wraps

Cut the fennel in half lengthwise and then slice as thinly as possible.

Place the sliced fennel in a bowl with the crabmeat, mayonnaise, salt and pepper, lemon zest and juice, and parsley. Mix well.

Set aside for 5 minutes to let the lemon juice wilt the fennel slightly.

Preheat a nonstick skillet or broiler pan until almost smoking, add the wraps, 1 at a time, and cook for 10 seconds on each side. This will add some color and soften the wraps.

Stir the filling mixture once and then divide it evenly among the wraps, placing some in the center of each wrap. Fold in each wrap at the ends, roll up, cut in half diagonally, and serve.

makes 8

about 1 lb/450 g firm-fleshed white fish, such as red snapper or cod

¼ tsp ground cumin

pinch of dried oregano

4 garlic cloves, very finely chopped

½ cup fish stock or water mixed with 1 fish bouillon cube

juice of ½ lemon or lime

8 flour tortillas

2–3 romaine lettuce leaves, shredded

2 ripe tomatoes, diced

salt and pepper

salsa, to serve

lemon halves, to garnish

fish burritos

Season the fish to taste with salt and pepper, then place in a pan with the cumin, oregano, garlic, and enough stock to cover.

Bring to a boil, then cook for 1 minute. Remove the pan from the heat. Let the fish cool in the cooking liquid for 30 minutes.

Remove the fish from the liquid with a slotted spoon and break up into bite-size pieces. Place in a nonmetallic bowl, sprinkle with the lemon juice, and set aside.

Heat the tortillas in an unoiled nonstick skillet, sprinkling them with a few drops of water as they heat. Wrap the tortillas in foil or a clean dish towel as you work to keep them warm.

Arrange the shredded lettuce in the middle of one tortilla, spoon on a few big chunks of the fish, then sprinkle with the tomatoes. Add some salsa and repeat with the other tortillas. Serve immediately garnished with lemon halves.

makes 4

½ cucumber

7 oz/200 g smoked mackerel, flaked

7 oz/200 g cream cheese

½ red onion finely chopped

1 tbsp horseradish

zest of 1 lemon

a small bunch of fresh dill, chopped

pepper

4 x 10-inch/25-cm wraps

smoked mackerel wraps with horseradish

Cut the cucumber in half lengthwise, scrape out the seeds with a spoon, and then chop into small dice.

Place the cucumber, mackerel, cream cheese, onion, and horseradish in a bowl and mix well. Add the lemon zest, dill, and pepper to taste.

Preheat a nonstick skillet or broiler pan until almost smoking, add the wraps, 1 at a time, and cook for 10 seconds on each side. This will add some color and soften the wraps.

Divide the mackerel mixture evenly among the wraps, spreading some evenly over each wrap. Fold in half 3 times to make a cone-shape and serve immediately.

makes 4

11 oz/310 g fresh tuna steak

1 tbsp olive oil

½ tsp cracked black pepper

½ tsp cumin seeds

4 x 10-inch/25-cm sun-dried
tomato wraps

salt

for the tabbouleh

¾ oz/20 g couscous

1 tbsp extra-virgin olive oil

1 tomato, chopped

1 scallion, finely chopped

a small bunch of fresh
flat-leaf parsley, shredded

salt and pepper

tuna & tabbouleh wraps

Rub the tuna with the olive oil and sprinkle with the pepper, cumin, and some salt.

Heat a nonstick broiler pan until almost smoking, add the tuna, and cook for 30 seconds on each side. Remove from the pan and set aside. If you prefer your tuna less rare, cook it for an additional 30 seconds on each side.

To make the tabbouleh, bring a tea kettle of water to a boil. Put the couscous and olive oil in a heatproof bowl, pour on enough boiling water to just cover the couscous, and set aside for 5 minutes.

Stir the couscous with a fork to separate the grains. If the couscous is still a little hard, add a little more boiling water and repeat the process.

Add the tomato, scallion, and parsley to the couscous and season with salt and pepper to taste.

makes 4

1 ripe avocado

7 oz/200 g cooked peeled shrimp

4 x 10-inch/25-cm wraps

4 Boston lettuce leaves

for the dressing

3 tbsp mayonnaise

1 tbsp tomato ketchup

1 tsp Worcestershire sauce

dash of Tabasco

salt and pepper

shrimp & avocado wraps

Halve the avocado, remove the pit, peel and cut into eighths.

To make the dressing, mix the mayonnaise, ketchup, Worcestershire sauce, and Tabasco sauce together in a bowl. Season with salt and pepper to taste. Add the shrimp and mix well.

Preheat a nonstick skillet or broiler pan until almost smoking, add the wraps, 1 at a time, and cook for 10 seconds on each side. This will add some color and soften the wraps.

To assemble the wraps, firstly place a lettuce leaf in the center of each wrap, then divide the shrimp in dressing evenly between them. Top with some avocado, then fold in the wraps at the ends, roll up, cut in half diagonally and serve.

Fresh from the Garden

makes 8

¹/₄ stick unsalted butter

¹/₂ tbsp sunflower-seed oil

7 oz/200 g leeks, halved, rinsed, and finely shredded

freshly grated nutmeg, to taste

1 tbsp finely snipped fresh chives

8 savory crêpes

3 oz/85 g soft goat cheese, rind removed if necessary, chopped

salt and pepper

leek & goat cheese crêpes

Melt the butter with the oil in a heavy-bottom skillet with a lid over medium-high heat. Add the leeks and stir around so that they are well coated. Stir in salt and pepper to taste, but remember the cheese might be salty. Add a few gratings of nutmeg, then cover the leeks with a sheet of wet waxed paper and put the lid on the skillet. Reduce the heat to very low and let the leeks sweat for 5–7 minutes until very tender, but not brown. Stir in the chives, then taste and adjust the seasoning if necessary.

Place 1 crêpe on the counter and put one eighth of the leeks on the crêpe. Top with one eighth of the cheese, then fold the crêpe into a square pocket or simply roll it around the filling. Fill and fold, or roll, the remaining crêpes in the same way.

Should you wish to serve the crêpes hot, preheat the oven to 400°F/200°C. Place the crêpes on a baking sheet in the oven and bake for 5 minutes, or until the crêpes are hot and the cheese starts to melt.

makes 4

1 red onion, cut into eighths

1 red pepper, seeded and
cut into eighths

1 small eggplant,
cut into eighths

1 zucchini, cut into eighths

4 tbsp extra-virgin olive oil

1 garlic clove, crushed

3 1/2 oz/100 g feta cheese,
crumbled

a small bunch of fresh mint,
shredded

4 x 10-inch/25-cm sun-dried
tomato wraps

salt and pepper

roasted vegetable & feta cheese wraps

Preheat the oven to 425°F/220°C.

Mix the vegetables, olive oil, garlic, and some salt and pepper together and place in the oven in a nonstick roasting pan. Cook for 15–20 minutes, or until golden and cooked through.

Remove from the oven and let cool. Mix in the cheese and the mint.

Preheat a nonstick skillet or broiler pan until almost smoking, add the wraps, 1 at a time, and cook for 10 seconds on each side. This will add some color and soften the wraps.

Divide the vegetable and cheese mixture evenly among the wraps, placing some along the center of each wrap. Fold in each wrap at the ends, roll up, cut in half, and serve.

makes 8

2 tbsp olive oil, for cooking

1 large onion, very finely chopped

8 oz/225 g small mushrooms, finely sliced

2 fresh mild green chiles, seeded and very finely chopped

2 garlic cloves, very finely chopped

5⅝ cups spinach leaves, torn into pieces if large

6 oz/175 g Cheddar cheese, grated

8 flour tortillas

vegetable oil, for deep-frying

spinach & mushroom chimichangas

Heat the oil in a large, heavy-bottom skillet. Add the onion and cook over medium heat for 5 minutes, or until softened.

Add the mushrooms, chiles, and garlic and cook for 5 minutes, or until the mushrooms are lightly browned. Add the spinach and cook, stirring, for 1–2 minutes, or until just wilted. Add the cheese and stir until just melted.

Meanwhile, to warm the tortillas, heat an unoiled nonstick skillet, add a tortilla, and heat through, sprinkling with a few drops of water as it heats. Wrap in foil or a clean dish towel to keep warm. Repeat with the other tortillas.

Spoon an equal quantity of the mixture into the center of each tortilla. Fold in 2 opposite sides of each tortilla to cover the filling, then roll up to enclose it completely.

Heat the oil for deep-frying in a deep-fryer or large, deep pan to 350–375°F/180–190°C, or until a cube of bread browns in 30 seconds. Deep-fry the chimichangas 2 at a time, turning once, for 5–6 minutes, or until crisp and golden. Drain on paper towels before serving.

makes 4

4 x 10-inch/25-cm wraps

4 cherry tomatoes, halved

1/2 cucumber, seeded and quartered

2 oz/55 g of baby spinach leaves

for the hummus

7 oz/200 g canned chickpeas, drained

1 garlic clove, crushed

4 tbsp extra-virgin olive oil

1 tsp tahini

1 tsp lemon juice

2 oz/55 g pitted green olives, chopped

a small bunch of flat-leaf parsley, shredded

salt and pepper

green olive hummus wraps

To make the hummus place the chickpeas, garlic, olive oil, tahini, and lemon juice in a food processor and blend until smooth. Season with salt and pepper to taste, transfer to a bowl and mix in the olives and parsley.

Preheat a nonstick skillet or broiler pan until almost smoking, add the wraps, 1 at a time, and cook for 10 seconds on each side. This will add some color and soften the wraps.

Spread some hummus over each wrap and divide the tomatoes, cucumber, and spinach among them, placing some in the center of each wrap. Fold in the wraps at the ends, roll up, cut in half diagonally, and serve.

makes 4

3¹/₂ oz/100 g green beans, trimmed

3¹/₂ oz/100 g canned borlotti beans, drained

3¹/₂ oz/100 g canned kidney beans drained

¹/₂ red onion, finely sliced

4 tbsp extra-virgin olive oil

1 tsp red wine vinegar

3¹/₂ oz/100 g cooked beet

1 ripe avocado

4 x 10-inch/25-cm herb wraps

salt and pepper

three-bean wraps

Bring a small saucepan of lightly salted water to a boil, add the green beans and blanch for 30 seconds, then place under cold running water, until cold. Drain and reserve.

Place the borlotti beans, kidney beans, onion, olive oil, and vinegar in a bowl, add the green beans and season with salt and pepper to taste.

Meanwhile, cut the beets into 1-inch/2.5-cm dice. Halve the avocado, remove the pit, then peel and chop it roughly. Add the beet and the avocado to the bean mixture and combine.

Preheat a nonstick skillet or broiler pan until almost smoking, add the wraps, 1 at a time, and cook for 10 seconds on each side. This will add some color and soften the wraps.

Divide the filling evenly among the wraps, placing some along the center of each wrap. Fold in each wrap at the ends, roll up, cut in half, and serve.

makes 4

10 oz/280 g sharp Cheddar
cheese, grated

5 oz/140 g chunky vegetable
piccalilli

4 scallions, chopped

salt and pepper

4 x 10-inch/25-cm wraps

cheddar & piccalilli wraps

Mix all the ingredients together and season with salt and pepper to taste.

Preheat a nonstick skillet or broiler pan until almost smoking, add the wraps, 1 at a time, and cook for 10 seconds on each side. This will add some color and soften the wraps.

Divide the mixture evenly among the wraps, placing some in the center of each. Fold in the wraps at the ends, roll up, cut in half, and serve.

makes 4

10 oz/280 g cooked beet, diced

3¹/₂ oz/100 g Roquefort cheese, crumbled

3¹/₂ oz/100 g walnuts, halved

1 tbsp mayonnaise

a small bunch of arugula

4 x 10-inch/25-cm multigrain wraps

pepper

beet & roquefort wraps

Mix the beet, Roquefort, walnuts, and mayonnaise together. Season with pepper to taste and gently add the arugula leaves.

Preheat a nonstick skillet or broiler pan until almost smoking, then add the wraps, 1 at a time, and cook for 10 seconds on each side. This will add some color and soften the wraps.

Divide the mixture evenly among the wraps, placing some in the center of each wrap. Fold in each wrap at the ends, roll up, cut in half, and serve.

makes 4

3 red onions, cut into eighths

3 tbsp extra-virgin olive oil

9 oz/250 g goat cheese, crumbled

3 1/2 oz/100 g slivered almonds, toasted

a small bunch of fresh flat-leaf parsley, shredded

4 x 10-inch/25-cm wraps

salt and pepper

goat cheese & caramelized onion wraps

Preheat the oven to 425°F/220°C.

Mix the onions and olive oil together and season with salt and pepper. Place on a nonstick baking sheet and cook in the oven for 15–20 minutes, until golden and cooked through. Remove from the oven and let cool.

Combine the onion mixture with the cheese, almonds, and parsley and set aside.

Preheat a nonstick skillet or broiler pan until almost smoking, add the wraps, 1 at a time, and cook for 10 seconds on each side. This will add some color and soften the wraps.

Divide the filling evenly among the wraps, spreading the mix evenly over the wrap. Fold in half 3 times to make a cone-shape and serve immediately.

makes 4

7 oz/200 g new potatoes, halved

4 eggs

1 small bunch of watercress

4 tbsp mayonnaise

1 tsp mustard

1 small white onion, finely chopped

4 x 10-inch/25-cm wraps

salt and pepper

egg & watercress wraps

Put the new potatoes in a small saucepan, cover with water, and add a small amount of salt. Bring to a boil, then simmer for 15 minutes, or until cooked. Drain and once cool, chop the potatoes into bite-size pieces.

Bring a small saucepan of water to a boil, add the eggs, and cook for 9 minutes, then cool under cold running water for 5 minutes. Shell the eggs and chop them roughly.

Roughly chop the watercress and then place it in a bowl with the potatoes, eggs, mayonnaise, mustard, and onion. Season with salt and pepper to taste, then mix until all ingredients are well combined.

Preheat a nonstick skillet or broiler pan until almost smoking, then add the wraps, 1 at a time, and cook for 10 seconds on each side. This will add some color and soften the wraps.

Divide the mixture among the wraps, placing some in the center of each wrap. Fold in each wrap at the ends, roll up, cut in half diagonally, and serve.

makes 4

4 x 10-inch/25-cm wraps

3 fresh buffalo mozzarella cheeses, drained and sliced

4 plum tomatoes, each one cut into eighths

a small bunch of arugula

for the pesto

2½ oz/70 g pine nuts

1 garlic clove, crushed

a small bunch of fresh basil

4 tbsp extra-virgin olive oil

2 1/2 oz/70 g Parmesan cheese, freshly grated

salt and pepper

mozzarella & pesto wraps

To make the pesto, put the pine nuts, garlic, and basil in a food processor, then process, adding the olive oil a tablespoon at a time. When the mixture is smooth, scrape into a bowl, then add the Parmesan cheese and the salt and pepper.

Preheat a nonstick skillet or broiler pan until almost smoking, then add the wraps, 1 at a time, and cook for 10 seconds on each side. This will add some color and soften the wraps.

Spread the pesto over the wraps.

Divide the slices of mozzarella cheese evenly among the wraps, placing some in the center of each wrap, then top with the tomatoes and the arugula. Fold in each wrap at the ends, roll up, cut into slices and serve.

All Things Sweet

makes 8–10

generous ⅔ cup all-purpose
flour

scant ¼ cup unsweetened
cocoa

pinch of salt

1 egg

2 tbsp superfine sugar

1½ cups milk

scant 2 tbsp unsalted butter

confectioners' sugar,
for dusting

ice cream or pouring cream,
to serve

for the berry compote

5½ oz/150 g fresh
blackberries

5½ oz/150 g fresh blueberries

8 oz/225 g fresh raspberries

generous ¼ cup superfine
sugar

juice of ½ lemon

½ tsp allspice (optional)

chocolate crêpes with berry compote

Preheat the oven to 275°F/140°C. Sift the flour, unsweetened cocoa, and salt together into a large bowl and make a well in the center.

Beat the egg, sugar, and half the milk together in a separate bowl, then pour the mixture into the dry ingredients. Beat the dry ingredients into the liquid, gradually drawing them in from the side, until a batter is formed. Gradually beat in the remaining milk. Pour the batter into a pitcher.

Heat a 7-inch/18-cm nonstick skillet over medium heat and add 1 teaspoon of the butter.

When the butter has melted, pour in enough batter to cover the bottom, then swirl it around the skillet so that you have a thin layer. Cook for 30 seconds and then lift the crêpe to check it is cooked. Loosen the edges of the crêpe, then flip it over. Cook on the other side until the bottom is golden brown.

Transfer the crêpe to a warmed plate and keep warm in the preheated oven while you cook the remaining batter, adding the remaining butter to the skillet as necessary. Make a stack of the crêpes with parchment paper in between each crêpe.

To make the compote, pick over the berries and put in a pan with the sugar, lemon juice, and allspice, if using. Cook over low heat until the sugar has dissolved and the berries are warmed through. Do not overcook.

Put a crêpe on a warmed serving plate and spoon some of the compote onto the center. Either roll or fold the crêpe and dust with confectioners' sugar. Repeat with the remaining crêpes. Serve with ice cream or pouring cream.

makes 8

8 sweet crêpes made with the finely grated rind of 1 lemon added to the batter

2 tbsp brandy

for the orange sauce

¼ cup superfine sugar

1 tbsp water

finely grated rind of 1 large orange

½ cup freshly squeezed orange juice

½ stick unsalted butter, diced

1 tbsp Cointreau, Grand Marnier, or other orange-flavored liqueur

crêpes suzette

To make the orange sauce, place the sugar in a wide sauté pan or skillet over medium heat and stir in the water. Continue stirring until the sugar dissolves, then increase the heat to high and let the syrup bubble for 1–2 minutes, or until it begins to turn golden brown.

Stir in the orange rind and juice, then add the butter and continue stirring until it melts. Stir in the orange-flavored liqueur.

Lay one of the crêpes flat in the sauté pan and spoon the sauce over. Using a fork and the spoon, fold the crêpe into quarters and push to the side of the pan. Add the next crêpe to the pan and repeat. Continue until all the crêpes are coated with the sauce and folded. Remove the pan from the heat.

Warm the brandy in a ladle or small pan, ignite and pour over the crêpes to flambé, while shaking the pan.

When the flames die down, serve the crêpes with the sauce spooned over.

makes 4

1 large mango, peeled and cut into large pieces

1 small pineapple, peeled, cored, and cut into large chunks

4 tbsp Greek-style yogurt

1 tbsp honey

4 x 10-inch/25-cm plain wraps

4 tbsp honey

1 tbsp butter, melted

1 tsp allspice

sweet & spicy wraps

Mix the mango, pineapple, yogurt, and honey together.

Preheat the broiler to high.

Brush the wraps with some honey and butter, sprinkle with allspice, then place under the broiler for 1 minute to color and soften the wraps.

Divide the fruit mixture evenly among the wraps, placing some down the center of each. Roll up the wraps and serve.

makes 8

3 large bananas

6 tbsp orange juice

grated rind of 1 orange

2 tbsp orange- or
banana-flavored liqueur

for the hot chocolate sauce

1 tbsp unsweetened cocoa

2 tsp cornstarch

3 tbsp milk

1 1/2 oz/40 g semisweet
chocolate, broken into pieces

1 tbsp butter

1/2 cup corn syrup

1/4 tsp vanilla extract

for the crêpes

3/4 cup all-purpose flour

1 tbsp unsweetened cocoa

1 egg

1 tsp sunflower oil

1 1/4 cups milk

oil, for frying

chocolate & banana crêpes

Peel and slice the bananas and arrange them in a dish with the orange juice and rind and the liqueur. Set aside.

Mix the unsweetened cocoa and cornstarch in a bowl, then stir in the milk. Put the chocolate in a pan with the butter and corn syrup. Heat gently, stirring until well blended. Add the cocoa mixture and bring to a boil over gentle heat, stirring. Simmer for 1 minute, then remove from the heat and stir in the vanilla extract.

To make the crêpes, sift the flour and unsweetened cocoa into a mixing bowl and make a well in the center. Add the egg and oil. Gradually whisk in the milk to form a smooth batter. Heat a little oil in a heavy-based skillet and pour off any excess. Pour in a little batter and tilt the skillet to coat the bottom. Cook over medium heat until the underside is browned. Flip over and cook the other side. Slide the crêpe out of the skillet and keep warm. Repeat until all the batter has been used.

To serve, reheat the chocolate sauce for 1–2 minutes. Fill the crêpes with the bananas and fold in half or into triangles. Pour over a little chocolate sauce and serve.

exotic fruit crêpes

makes 8

for the batter

generous 1 cup
all-purpose flour

pinch of salt

1 egg

1 egg yolk

1¼ cups coconut milk

4 tsp vegetable oil,
plus extra for frying

for the filling

1 banana

1 papaya

juice of 1 lime

2 passion fruits

1 mango, peeled, pitted,
and sliced

4 lychees, pitted and halved

1–2 tbsp honey

flowers or fresh mint sprigs,
to decorate

Sift the flour and salt into a bowl. Make a well in the center and add the egg, egg yolk, and a little of the coconut milk. Gradually draw the flour into the egg mixture, beating well and gradually adding the remaining coconut milk to form a smooth batter. Stir in the oil. Cover and chill for 30 minutes.

Peel and slice the banana and place in a bowl. Peel and slice the papaya, discarding the seeds. Add to the banana with the lime juice and mix well. Cut the passion fruit in half and scoop out the flesh and seeds into the fruit bowl. Stir in the mango, lychees, and honey.

Heat a little oil in a 6-inch/15-cm skillet. Pour in just enough of the crêpe batter to cover the bottom of the skillet and tilt so that it spreads thinly and evenly. Cook until the crêpe is just set and the underside is lightly browned, turn, and briefly cook the other side. Remove from the skillet and keep warm. Repeat with the remaining batter to make a total of 8 crêpes.

To serve, place a little of the prepared fruit filling along the center of each crêpe and then roll it into a cone shape. Lay on warmed serving plates, decorate with flowers or mint sprigs, and serve.

makes 8

11 1/2 oz/325 g ricotta cheese

3/4 cup milk

4 eggs, separated

1 cup all-purpose flour

1 tsp baking powder

pinch of salt

2 oz/55 g milk chocolate, grated

2 tbsp butter

for the toffee orange sauce

4 tbsp sweet butter

3 oz/85 g brown sugar

2/3 cup heavy cream

2–3 tbsp orange juice or Cointreau

chocolate chip crêpes

To make the toffee orange sauce, melt the butter with the brown sugar in a pan over low heat until the sugar has melted, stir in the cream, and bring to a boil. Simmer for 3–4 minutes. Remove from the heat and stir in the orange juice or Cointreau. Set aside.

To make the crêpes, put the ricotta cheese, milk, and egg yolks in a mixing bowl and stir well. Sift in the flour, baking powder, and salt, add the chocolate and mix well.

Whisk the egg whites until stiff, then fold into the ricotta mixture.

Heat a nonstick skillet and wipe with a little of the butter. Spoon in 2 tablespoons of the batter and cook for 2–3 minutes until bubbles appear, then flip the crêpe over and cook for an additional 2–3 minutes. Repeat with a little more butter each time until you have 8 crêpes. Serve with the sauce poured over.

makes 4

10½ oz/300 g apples, peeled
and cored

2 oz/55 g golden raisins

2 tbsp brown sugar

1 tsp cinnamon

4 sheets filo pastry

4 tbsp butter, melted

confectioners' sugar,
for dusting

warm filo wraps with spiced apples

Preheat the oven to 400°F/200°C. Cut the apples into 1-inch/2.5-cm pieces and mix with the golden raisins, brown sugar, and cinnamon.

Lay out the filo sheets and brush with melted butter, reserving a little. Fold each sheet in half and brush once more with butter.

Divide the apple mixture among the filo sheets, placing some in the center of one end of each. Fold in each side, then roll into a cylinder shape. Brush with the reserved melted butter and dust with the confectioners' sugar.

Place in the oven on a nonstick baking sheet and cook for 10 minutes, or until golden.

Divide the wraps among 4 plates and serve.

makes 4

½ tbsp vegetable oil

2 oz/55 g blanched almonds

½ oz/15 g pistachios

5 oz/150 g clear honey

3½ oz/100 g dried
bread crumbs

zest of ½ orange

4 x round sheets Asian rice
paper

rice paper wraps with pistachios & almonds

Heat the oil in a skillet, add the almonds, and fry them until they start to brown, then add the pistachios. Remove the nuts from the skillet when golden brown.

Heat the honey in a small saucepan over low heat; add the nuts, bread crumbs, and orange zest.

Stir continually for 5 minutes, until the mixture has thickened to a paste. Remove the pan from the heat and let cool.

Place the rice papers on a flat surface and brush with warm water—they will soften and become pliable after a few minutes.

Divide the nut mixture evenly among the rice papers, placing some along the center of each paper in a cylinder shape. Fold over the ends of the rice papers, roll up carefully, and serve.

makes 4

3½ oz/100 g dried figs, chopped

3½ oz/100 g dried dates, chopped

½ oz/15 g preserved ginger in syrup, chopped

2 tbsp ginger syrup

7 oz/220 g sushi rice

1¼ cups water

1 tbsp rice vinegar

1 tbsp sugar

sweet sushi wraps

In a large bowl, mix the figs, dates, ginger, and ginger syrup together. Set aside to infuse for 10 minutes.

Wash the rice in a strainer under cold running water, until the water runs clear.

Add the water to the rice in a nonstick heavy-bottom saucepan, bring to a boil, then reduce the heat to low and cook, covered, until all of the water has disappeared. This will take about 6 minutes. Remove from the heat and let stand for 15 minutes.

Stir the vinegar and sugar into the rice.

Place a sushi mat on a flat surface and cover with a layer of plastic wrap.

Using wet fingers place half the rice on the mat, spreading it out evenly until it covers the mat.

Place half the filling along the center of the rice.

Lift up the edge of the mat closest to you and slowly roll it away from you in a smooth movement until you have formed a cylinder shape, applying gentle pressure to keep it neat and compact.

Repeat the process with the remaining rice and filling.

Cut off the ends of the wraps, cut in half, and serve.

makes 4

7 oz/200g dried apricots

5 1/2 oz/150 g rhubarb,
roughly chopped

10 fl oz/300 ml water

2 1/2 oz/70g granulated sugar

confectioners' sugar,
for dusting

heavy cream, to serve

for the calzone

8 oz/225g all-purpose flour,
plus extra for dusting

1/2 tsp salt

1/2 tsp active dry yeast

1/2 cup milk

4 tbsp warm water

1 tsp olive oil, plus extra for
brushing

sweet filled calzone with apricots & rhubarb

Place the apricots, rhubarb, water, and granulated sugar in a heavy-bottom saucepan and cook over low heat for 15–20 minutes. Remove the pan from the heat and let cool.

To make the calzone, sift the flour and salt into a bowl; add the yeast, milk, and water. Mix with your hands until well combined, turn out onto a floured counter, and knead for 5 minutes or until silky. Using your fingers, make indentations in the dough and pour over the olive oil. Mix thoroughly until all of the oil has been absorbed.

Shape the dough into a ball and place in a clean bowl, brush with oil, then cover with plastic wrap. Let stand at room temperature for 1–1½ hours or until the dough has doubled in size.

Preheat the oven to its highest setting, then put a heavy nonstick baking sheet in the oven for preheating.

Divide the dough into 4 even-size pieces on a floured counter and roll into thin pancakes. Divide the filling evenly among the calzone, placing some along the center of each. Brush the dough with water and fold over, pinching at the edges. Dust with confectioners' sugar and serve with heavy cream on the side.